Freedom from Sinful Thoughts

Freedom from Sinful Thoughts

J. Heinrich Arnold

Foreword by John Michael Talbot

 The Plough Publishing House

© 1997 by The Plough Publishing House
The Bruderhof Foundation

Farmington PA 15437 USA
Robertsbridge, East Sussex, TN32 5DR England

First Printing: 1973
Second Printing: 1986

Second Edition: 1997

06 05 04 03 02 01   10 9 8 7 6 5

Cover photograph: Duncan McNicol / Tony Stone Images

Arnold's quotes from Baudouin are translated from Charles Baudouin, *Suggestion und Autosuggestion: Psychologisch-Pädogogische Untersuchungen.*..(Dresden: Sibyllen Verlag, 1925). The excerpts from Eckhardt are from Otto Karrer, *Meister Eckehart Spricht* (Munich: Verlag Ars Sacra/Josef Mueller, 1925).

Library of Congress Cataloging-in-Publication Data

Arnold, J. Heinrich, 1913–
    Freedom from sinful thoughts / J. Heinrich Arnold : foreword by
John Michael Talbot. -- 2nd ed.
        p.   cm.
    ISBN: 0-87486-094-6 (pbk.)
    1. Spiritual life--Christianity.   2. Thought and thinking.
3. Temptation.   4. Sin.   I. Title.
BV4509. 5. A74 1997
248 . 4--DC2I   97-31609
                                                                     CIP

Printed in the USA

IF anyone is thirsty
let him come to me and drink.
If anyone believes in me...
streams of living water shall flow
from out his body.

Jesus of Nazareth

To the Reader

Johann Christoph Arnold

ALTHOUGH twenty-four years have passed since the publication of my father's first book, *Freedom from Sinful Thoughts,* I remember the occasion vividly. He had worked on the book for months, and even though it was a slim little volume, much love, energy, and thought went into it. I had already been working with him in the ministry for two years, but the project of putting together the book cemented our relationship in a wonderful way.

One thing always seemed to concern my father in a special way: the pastoral task of counseling, comforting, and encouraging members of the community who were going through a particular struggle or a hard time. For him, *Freedom from Sinful Thoughts* was a book that *had* to be written: he had seen too many people whose struggles dragged on in endless frustration or despair, and he wanted to share his conviction that there was a way out.

Even before the book appeared in print, it found an amazing echo among readers; using the unfinished manuscript as an outline, he held a series of talks on the struggle for a pure heart. The response was unexpected: letters poured in, and it soon became clear that even if this was not a topic of conversation, it was certainly one of widespread concern, and not only among new or younger believers, but among mature, committed Christians as well.

Once the book was published, the flood of letters only increased. Strangers and prison inmates wrote, telling my father that the book had been a turning point in their lives, or that it had given them new courage. More than one person claimed that reading it had saved them from committing suicide. And the book sold, without fanfare, but steadily — year after year.

My father died in 1982, and in the years since, many unpublished materials have come to light and been made accessible: tapes, transcripts, notes, outlines, and volumes and volumes of letters. If this new edition appears unrecognizable to readers familiar with the first edition, it is because the original text has been reorganized and vastly amplified in order to make use of these sources. The heart of the book — my father's insistence that Christ brings relief from struggle, healing from the wounds of evil, and freedom from the bondage of sin — remains unchanged.

Freedom from Sinful Thoughts contains significant insights into a universal and most crucial struggle, in language simple enough for anyone to understand. More than that, it holds out the promise of new life to readers whose self-concern, secret sins, and feelings of guilt or fear block their prayers and keep them from loving God and their neighbor

with a free and undivided heart. In a world that
often seems dark enough to make one despair, it
carries a message of joy and hope.

Rifton, New York
August 1997

Contents

Foreword

John Michael Talbot

THE CHRISTIAN tradition is filled with wisdom concerning the handling of thoughts and emotions, and J. Heinrich Arnold's *Freedom from Sinful Thoughts* is a wonderful example. In a manner not unlike St. Augustine in the West, and the monastic fathers of the East, Arnold confronts the realities of battling temptation and sin from his own communal tradition. His insights are honest and realistic, yet they are infused with an uncompromising faith in the Spirit's power to renew and transform.

We are what we think. This is why we should never underestimate what we allow to enter our minds. It is by means of thoughts that the spirits of evil wage a secret war on the soul. Thus the fifth-century bishop Maximus warns us, "Just as it is easier to sin in the mind than in action, so warfare through our impassioned conceptual images of things is harder than warfare through things themselves."

Jesus says, "From the thoughts of the heart stem evil designs." He also says, "Wherever your treasure lies, there your heart will be." For too many of us, including those of us who call ourselves Christians, our private thoughts or fantasies are our treasure. We do not want to sin, but we do not want to give up our private fantasies either. Yet it is precisely in our thought-life where the struggle for good and evil is won or lost. The Apostle Paul understood this and so wrote: "Be transformed by the renewing of your mind; then you will be able to test and approve what God's will is — his good, pleasing, and perfect will" (Rom. 12:1–2). For Paul, the transformation of our actions begins with the transformation of our thoughts — that is,

freedom from sinful thoughts is paramount to
freedom in Christ.

Arnold's attention to sinful thoughts must be seen in this greater context of transformation. His is not a morbid preoccupation with perfection. All of us struggle with unwanted images and thoughts. But as Arnold assures us, tempting thoughts are not in and of themselves sinful. It is what we do with them that matters. James says, "Once passion has conceived, it gives birth to sin." Therefore the question is, Do we nurture the evil thoughts that come to us, linger on them, and so feed them; or do we take them up as in a battle and strive to overcome them in Christ?

It is Christ who alone breaks the curse of sin. It is he who gives the struggle meaning – for he is the purpose and goal of all our striving. Therefore Augustine writes, "Let us sing alleluias here on earth...even here amidst trials and temptations and anxiety…not in order to enjoy a life of leisure, but in order to lighten our labors." It is by praising God in the midst of temptation that we will be freed of heaviness within our souls.

In the end, our struggle is a joyful one. Even when we fail — and we will — we have the assurance that God's rule of love is greater than our hearts and minds. And further, we can have, as Arnold urges us, "absolute trust in Jesus, so that even if we feel nothing yet, we will give ourselves absolutely and without reserve to him with all we are and have…Then he will give us forgiveness, cleansing, and peace of heart; and these lead to a love that cannot be described."

To be freed from sinful thoughts is a great gift, a gift of God's love that every reader may experience in pondering the wisdom of this book. Without it, we are left floundering in frustration. With it, we are more than conquerors.

Eureka Springs, Arkansas
September 1997

I The Struggle

THE PROBLEM of sinful thoughts concerns
every believer at one time or another. For the man
or woman who is repeatedly plagued with unwanted feelings or images, however, it is a special
burden. Every idea presses for realization, and this
is a curse if the idea is an evil one. I know of
people who, when troubled by an evil desire or
idea, would rather die than allow it to become
reality — and yet this resolve seems unable to spare
them struggle; it is as if they are pursued by the
idea. With some it is a matter of envy, spite, or
mistrust; with others, sexual fantasies; with still
others, hatred, blasphemy, or even murder.

I doubt if anyone can really explain what goes on
in his or her own heart. God alone knows the state
of each soul. But we do know that according to
the Gospel, "wicked thoughts proceed from the

heart," and that it also says, "Blessed are they whose hearts are pure." These simple words of Jesus are fundamental to understanding this book.

I have counseled many men and women who are afraid to admit that they struggle with unwanted thoughts; they think they are the only ones afflicted by such things. Actually, in a certain sense, all of us have an evil nature. All of us can, at one time or another in our lives, succumb to the devil, who is not just an abstract idea, but a real force of evil who attacks each person at his or her weakest point. Once the devil wins a place in our heart, the evil that takes root there may lead to words, which in turn will lead to deeds.

As a child growing up in Germany in the 1920s, I heard hateful remarks against the Jews, especially at the *Gasthaus* across the road from my parents' house. Most people in the village brushed the anti-semitism aside, but my father protested it vehemently: "It may only be evil talk now, but it will lead to evil deeds. One day they will really do what they say." And they did.

Some people are so frequently beset by evil thoughts that they live in what can only be called torment. They, too, must trust that God sees deeper into the heart. God surely recognizes that despite the wavering of our imagination, our inmost heart does not want the evil thoughts burdening us. And if we remain unsure even of that, we can take comfort in the words of the 13th century mystic Eckhart, who writes: "In order to be set aflame by God's love, you must long for God. If you cannot yet feel this longing, then long for the longing." Clearly, any longing for purity, however new or undefined, is the beginning of God's working in the heart.

There is, of course, a significant difference between deliberately entertaining evil thoughts and struggling against them. I have counseled people who felt so hounded by unwanted thoughts or desires that they told me they would walk around the whole earth, if they could, to be freed of them. They would give anything to find peace of mind and a pure heart.

Such determination is good, but it is important to recognize at the same time that we cannot liberate ourselves in our own strength. The struggle between good and evil is not only something "in the mind," but a battle of cosmic proportions between sin, which Paul calls "another law at work in the members of our flesh," and the Spirit. To win this fight demands faith in Jesus, who promises us victory "wherever two or three gather in my name."

Many Christians do not believe in the reality of this fight, let alone in the reality of evil. This book will be of no use to them. Rather, it is intended

for those who have known sin, who earnestly seek
to be freed of its weight, and who long for purity
of heart.

As a subject for a book, "sinful thoughts" is not
a fashionable one; yet I have come to see, over many
years, that it is something thousands of people
battle with. If this little book can help guide even
one of them toward the freedom of the cross, it
will have served its purpose.

II

Temptation

WHERE DOES temptation end and sin begin?
If we are plagued or tempted by evil thoughts, that
in itself is not sinning. For instance, if we feel
tempted to lash out at someone who has wronged
us, yet then find strength to forgive him, we have
not sinned. But if we refuse to let go of our hurt
and hold a grudge against him, that is sin. In the
same way, if we are aroused by a lustful thought
but reject it, we have not sinned. Naturally it is
quite different if we willingly pursue that thought,
for instance by buying a pornographic magazine.

It is always a question of what we do when
temptation comes. Martin Luther once wrote that
evil thoughts come like birds flying over our heads.
We cannot help that. But if we allow them to
build nests on our heads, then we are responsible
for them.

We will never be completely free of temptation; we should not even expect it. Even Jesus was tempted. Satan came to him in the wilderness disguised as an angel, and used words from scripture to tempt him – and only after the third temptation did Jesus recognize him and say, "Be gone from me, Satan! For scripture says, 'Worship the Lord your God and serve him alone.'" When the devil realized that he had been recognized, he left Jesus; and then angels came to Him and brought Him food (Mt. 4:10–11).

At one time the idea of Jesus being tempted *like an ordinary human being* seemed blasphemous to me. Yet there is no question: he was, although he never sinned. This is of crucial importance, in the first place for our own inner lives, but also in the way we treat others who battle severe temptations:

> As we children share in flesh and blood, he himself likewise partook of the same nature, that through death he might destroy him who has the power of

death, that is, the devil, and deliver all those who through fear of death were subject to lifelong bondage. For surely it is not with angels that he is concerned but with the descendants of Abraham. Therefore he had to be made like his brethren in every respect, so that he might become a merciful and faithful high priest in the service of God, to make expiation for the sins of the people. And because he himself has suffered and been tempted, he is able to help those who are tempted (Heb. 2:14–18).

The writer of the Letter is so concerned that this is clear to the reader, that he says it again in chapter 4, verse 15:

We do not have a high priest who is unable to sympathize with our weaknesses, but one who in every respect has been tempted as we are, yet without sinning.

Jesus never sinned. Even in the severest battle of his life — at Gethsemane, where he must have contended with forces of darkness beyond our power to imagine, with whole armies of evil spirits fighting for his heart – he never swerved from his love to his Father. He remained obedient and loyal.

For us, the struggle against darkness in our hearts will remain as long as we live. That is the bitter truth, and it means that we can never overcome the evil besetting us with our own strength. The issue is not merely thoughts, feelings, or images, but warring spirits – Paul calls them "powers, authorities, and potentates of darkness." We will need to pray for God's protection again and again; and when temptations come in spite of our prayers, we will have to ask for an answer to each of them. Yet there is no reason to despair:

> No temptation has seized you except what is common to man. And God is faithful; he will not let you be tempted beyond what you can bear. But when you are tempted, he will also provide a way of escape so that you can stand up under it (1 Cor. 10:13).

No one of us will ever have to undergo a battle
as desperate as the one Jesus fought for us on the
cross. In this struggle he took the full weight of
our condition, including temptation, upon himself
in order to redeem us. Temptation is not sin.

III

Deliberate Sin

IT IS ONE thing to be tormented by ideas or images we do not want, but quite another to pursue them intentionally. People who deliberately watch violent films or read pornographic literature for the pleasure it gives them are not simply struggling with temptation; they are sinning. I am assuming, in what I write, that the reader does not *want* those things he knows to be evil!

When we willingly entertain an evil thought, we are playing with forces of darkness whose power we may be unaware of. It is easy (and commonplace) to shrug off this idea; people say, "It doesn't hurt anyone, does it?" or "It's all in your head..." Yet there is a reason for the saying, "Thoughts are giants" – they press toward concrete realization, and if they are evil thoughts, they will lead to evil deeds. As James writes, "Temptation arises when a man is enticed and lured away by his own lust; then lust conceives, and gives birth to sin; and sin full-grown breeds death" (Jas. 1:14–15).

A horror like genocide does not happen overnight; it is the fruit of evil that has started in the mind. The Holocaust, for instance, was preceded by centuries of prejudice and slander, not to mention pogroms and other forms of persecution. The riots that swept America's large cities in the 1960s, too, were the result of smoldering racial hatreds that had persisted for hundreds of years. Study after study has shown a link between violent sex crimes and the films that perpetrators confess to having watched beforehand. Such "copycat crimes" show more blatantly than anything that the most heinous deeds have their root in the heart and mind.

As a young man, I knew Germans who had been quite harmless before the rise of Nazism —"nor-

mal" people with "good" characters — but who
were later gripped and driven by a spirit of evil.
And even though there were many who died pro-
testing this evil, the majority willingly gave in to it,
whether by becoming active participants in the
mass murder of the Jews, or by supporting Hitler
in other ways, even if only with silent indifference.
It was not a matter of just a few men ruling over a
nation: millions of people willingly submitted to
forces of demonic darkness.

Most often, of course, deliberate sin takes place
on a more personal level. One area of special concern to me as a pastor is the occult, which I have
run into often in my counseling work. Occultism
is often regarded as just another science to be stud-
ied. Yet supposedly harmless forms of spiritualism,
as well as superstitious practices such as wearing
health rings, tipping tables, or talking with the
dead, can bind a person to demonic forces even
when entered innocently. I firmly believe we should

reject these things completely. They have nothing to do with a childlike faith in Jesus.

I know there are people who study evil — people who try to discover its root and who attempt to unearth the secrets of Satan. This may be understandable, but is it godly? It seems to me that too many men and women in our society are already burdened by what they know of murder, fornication, and other sins.

Others willingly flirt with evil in the name of experimentation. These people try, in effect, to understand its arguments; they claim to reject darkness, but through toying with it, they are gripped more firmly by its power than they realize.

As long as we allow ourselves the loophole of indecision — as long as we give evil even a little rein in our hearts and do not break with it fully, we will never become wholly free; it will continue to exert power over us. I am not speaking only of the occult here, but of everything that is opposed to

God: jealousy, hatred, lust, the desire for power over other people, and all the other sins. As long as we deliberately steel even a small part of our hearts against God's intervention in our lives, we cut ourselves off from the mercy he offers us through Jesus.

Certainly a divided soul must be treated with compassion — Jesus himself says he will not "break a bruised reed" or "snuff a smoldering wick." But it is also clear, I believe, that ultimately he cannot tolerate anything that grieves the Holy Spirit. Jesus was and is fully victorious over the devil and his demons, and he demands our wholehearted service in the fight against them too.

IV   The Will

IN A STRUGGLE against temptation, what can
we do to blot out the evil clouding our inner eye,
or bring into focus the love of God we are looking
for? In the boxing ring or on the street, the strong-
willed man may be the winner; yet in the struggle
of the human heart, will power may have nothing
to do with the outcome of a battle.

It is impossible to defeat one's sinful nature by
will power alone, because the will is never wholly
free, but bent this way and that by conflicting
emotions and other forces at work on it. In an
inner struggle it becomes, as the German philoso-
phers say, especially *verkrampft* or "cramped," and
to enlist it may be of no use at all. In fact, it may
end up entrenching in our mind the very evil we
are struggling to overcome, or even drive it to

the point of becoming reality. In the words of the Swiss-French psychiatrist Charles Baudouin:

> When an idea imposes itself on the mind...all conscious efforts the subject makes in order to counteract it are not merely without the desired effect, but will actually go in the opposite direction and intensify it...with the result that the dominant idea is reinforced.

Paul writes knowingly of the problem:

> I do not understand what I do. For what I do I do not want to do, but what I hate to do...I have the desire to do what is good, but I cannot carry it out...(Rom. 7:15–17).

Perhaps it is helpful here to distinguish between the will and the deeper, essential longing of our heart: the conscience. Whereas the will reacts to temptation by attempting to inhibit the imagination and desire, the conscience (the early Quakers called it the "inner light") points us to true purity of heart. It is a guide in the innermost recesses of the soul, where Christ himself dwells. And when it takes the upper hand, the worst temptations can be overcome.

In examining the war of these two "wills," the question naturally arises, Where does all this unwanted evil come from? The only answer is to admit that the evil comes from our hearts. (I do not mean to deny that we are often attacked by evil — only to warn that to emphasize the role of the devil can be unhealthy. Ultimately, each of us must take responsibility for our thoughts and actions.) When we recognize this it is not difficult to understand why we are incapable of overcoming evil thoughts by means of our own will power, and we will humbly admit that we cannot cleanse our hearts in our own strength.

Again, as long as we try to conquer evil by sheer will power, evil will get the better of us. To quote

Baudouin's colleague Emil Coué, "when the will and the imagination are at war, the imagination gains the upper hand without exception." Yet as soon as we give ear to that innermost longing of heart that cries out for Jesus, the evil in us will retreat. And if we trust in this deeper will and pray, "Not my will, but your will, Jesus: your purity is greater than my impurity; your generosity will overcome my envy; your love will triumph over my hatred," it will gradually subside altogether.

We must believe: Jesus really *is* faithful to us, even though we are unfaithful, and he is not a distant Savior who reaches down from above, but a man who, as Paul writes, died on the cross "in human weakness," and now lives "by the power of God:"

> We, too, are weak as He was; but sharing this with Him, we shall be filled with life by the power of God, and you shall experience that!
>
> See to it that you are living the life of faith; put yourselves to the test! Or do you not notice that Jesus

Christ lives in you? You would otherwise not be
genuine in your faith. That we are genuine and have
been equal to the test, I hope you will come to see.
But we pray to God that He may protect you against
all evil. We are not concerned that we ourselves are
vindicated, but that you do what is right, even if we
should seem to be discredited. For we have no power
to act against the truth, but only for it. We indeed
rejoice if we are weak and you are strong. And my
whole prayer to God is that you allow yourselves to
be put back on the right road (2 Cor. 13:4–9).

V The Power of Suggestion

SHORTLY after my father's death I found, in his library, an old, yellowed volume by Baudouin (see p. 17 above), *Suggestion und Autosuggestion,* which I have often turned to when grappling with the whole issue of burdensome thoughts. According to Baudouin, suggestion may be briefly defined as the force that presses an idea toward realization through feelings and images that enter the subconscious from an external source:

> The idea of a pleasure or a pain, the idea of a feeling, tends to become this very pleasure, this pain, or this feeling...The sight of the sun, which arouses the thought of warmth, is sufficient to give the sensation of warmth as well; in contrast, the sight of snow and the reading of a thermometer outside awakens the idea of coldness.

The power of suggestion exerts itself on us every day, and at all times: each of us is subject to the influences of those we live and work with, for instance. There is also the more subtle — but equally powerful — force of suggestion through inanimate objects: the books, magazines, and newspapers we read, the shows and films we watch, the music we listen to, the advertisements and commercials that bombard us daily.

Obviously, suggestion can be a positive as well as negative force. Yet with regard to the struggle against unwanted thoughts, it is important to recognize just how powerfully it can work against the voice of the conscience. On a broader level, its negative power is evident in contemporary stances on divisive issues such as abortion and homosexuality, and also in our society's attitudes toward violence. Often these things arouse such strong feelings in people that it becomes impossible for them to speak about them objectively. How different it would be if each of us searched our own heart about these important questions rather than letting ourselves be swayed by what the media or the experts say!

The zeitgeist is most visible, perhaps, in the frightening shamelessness that marks our age. It shows itself in dress, literature, art, and music — through their expressions of inner disunity and separation from the Creator, and through their appeal to the lowest human instincts. At a deeper level, it can be seen elsewhere too: in government and corporate corruption, in the breakdown of the family and personal relationships, in schools and universities, in the mass media, in the worlds of medicine and law, and worst of all, in the emptiness and hypocrisy of the spiritual fare offered by so many churches.

Jesus' stance toward all this is clear: he condemns the "spirit of the age" and exposes it as the spirit of Satan, the "accuser of our brother" and

24   the "murderer from the beginning." And in doing
      so, he calls us to ask ourselves, "Where, amid all
      the divisiveness and noise of our time, is the still
      small voice of God?"

Autosuggestion

IN CONTRAST to suggestion, autosuggestion is "the releasing of a reflexive power of the imagination from within in response to external influences" (Baudouin).

Autosuggestion may seem like a positive force, and insofar as it helps us to substitute "good" mental images for "bad" ones, it is. Yet in my experience it is often not so simple. Sometimes the very fear of an evil idea triggers that idea and calls it to the fore. That, too, is autosuggestion. In this way, even against our will, we can work ourselves up into such a terrible state of inner tension that we no longer see a way out, and lose sight not only of God, but even our own resolve to come through the struggle.

Autosuggestion affects other areas of life as well. Anyone who has learned to ride a bicycle will remember making every mental effort to go to one side of the road to steer away from a ditch or a wall, but ending up in the ditch or the wall anyway. Why is this? Despite every effort of our will to avoid calamity (or is it because of our intense concentration?), there arises through autosuggestion the feeling that we *cannot* avoid it.

Baudouin illustrates this problem in the following passage and indicates the strenuousness — and certain failure — of attempting to overcome certain unwanted thoughts with other thoughts:

> A person is afraid at not being able to recall to mind a well-known name; he is shocked about the disobedience of his memory. Involuntarily, unconsciously, he makes a suggestion, which only aggravates the loss of memory. The more he strains to think of the name again, the deeper into this forgetfulness he sinks... Here we have the very distinct feeling that the more we strain, the more the name escapes us. Each renewed effort seems to darken the waters of our memory

more and more, seems to stir up ever thicker clouds
of mud from the bottom, as it were; in the end it is
all dark, and we see nothing anymore. Just a moment
ago we had the name on the tip of our tongue; now
it is lost again.

How do such losses of memory come about? Let
us assume that the lapse of memory just described,
with its accompanying angry dissatisfaction (possibly
unacknowledged), has been repeated several times.
Immediately the idea arises that our memory is fail-
ing. And it will in fact go downhill, but merely because we have thought so, because this forgetfulness
has made a strong impression on us, and because,
through that, our attention clings to the idea of
forgetfulness.

There is no doubt that many things enter our
minds as undeveloped thought-seeds which continue to work in our subconscious long after we
have dismissed them from our attention. One need
only think of the unwanted fantasies, especially

sexual ones, that beset every person at one time or another. Often such a fantasy develops from an image that originally held one's attention for only a brief moment. On the opposite side of the coin, we ought to remember the Old Testament story of Jacob, who kept his heart centered on prayer to God and was blessed with the most wonderful dream.

Baudouin's lines should be a warning to each of us about what we fill our minds and hearts with, especially before we go to sleep. I do not mean to lead the reader into further anxiety or self-concern; too many people seem inclined to over-analyze themselves already. But it is always a healthy thing to be able to face one's own shortcomings squarely. The Apostle Paul goes so far as to say that he who examines himself will not be judged.

The important thing is that our self-judgment is accompanied by faith in Christ, who wants to free

us from sin. Without this faith, preoccupation
with self may cause us to begin doubting our every
motive and to lose hope in the possibility of
change. Eventually it can cause such depression
that it leads us completely away from God.

In all of this, my main point is simply that an
understanding of autosuggestion, even if simpli-
fied or incomplete, should lead us to a sense of
responsibility. Armed with it, we can seek to re-
build those weak points in our inner lives where
the devil attacks us, and in this way free our ener-
gies for love.

When we use up all our energy in keeping our
inner lives above water, we have no strength left to
look beyond our struggles — no strength left to
love others. There is only one solution: to turn
away from our anxieties, and toward Jesus and our
brothers and sisters. If we do this, we will find that
he is not so unmerciful that we need live in con-

30   stant fear and self-circling. God is a God of love,
        and he gives hope and new life to all who seek
        him.

VII   Fascination

MOST people have experienced, at one time or another, the frustration of simply not being able to escape a thought. If it is merely a song that keeps going through our mind, or a positive or neutral image, the problem is just that: frustration. But when it is an evil idea, our inability to throw it off, no matter what we do, may drive us into great inner need. For some people, it is a question of envy or jealousy; others are tormented by mistrust and spiteful thoughts; still others seem to struggle unendingly with lustful images and ideas.

We have seen that anxiety over any thought plaguing us — and misplaced hopes of overcoming such a thought by focusing on other "counter-thoughts" — can lead us in only one direction: in a downward spiral of emotional confusion. In fact, I have seen that those who try hardest to "will" themselves into a Christlike frame of mind are sometimes plagued by the worst ideas: thoughts of blasphemy and murder.

What, then, can be done? In my experience, two things are important. First, we should remember that we are not alone in our struggle. It is easy to forget this, especially when our inner struggle is long or intense. But from what I have seen over years of counseling people, the struggle is a universal one, and may be overcome at least in part by sharing it with someone the afflicted person trusts, whether a pastor or priest, a spouse, a mentor, or a close friend.

Second, we must remain reassured that there *is* a way out. Once we give in to the demons of self-doubt and fear, the battle has already been lost. Baudouin writes:

> Since our attention returns again and again to this point of fascination, we imagine that we are no

longer able to divert it from this object. Next, this idea so far materializes that we no longer believe that we are able to become free. Here we have suggestion at work. And now in fact we cannot do anything different. Quite involuntarily we have accomplished a suggestion of powerlessness in ourselves.

The feeling of paralysis or powerlessness in the face of evil lies, I believe, close to being possessed. It may even *be* possession. One needs to exercise caution in using the word – there is a state in which we might feel besieged by evil spirits, yet do not let them take full possession of us. What the New Testament calls possession comes about when a person is completely dominated by the power of evil. But we must recognize that there *are* people today in such a condition.

In a world where everything is explained away by psychology and psychiatry, it seems tempting to dismiss the idea of possession. We have a medical label for every ill and, it seems, a cure. Yet there are so many people for whom psychiatry is ultimately of no help! I have often wondered what would happen if Jesus were to visit our overflowing mental hospitals. How many people would he recognize as possessed? How many men and women would he find beyond human help, desperately in need of *his* freeing touch?

In the end, whether a person is possessed by evil spirits or merely pursued by them, the same truth applies: only Christ, by means of his Holy Spirit, can drive away their darkness, sadness, and fear. For those of us who are free from the torments of fascination, this recognition should help us to treat those who are bound by them with special patience and compassion. For the person trapped in struggle, it means turning to Christ so that he can take the steering wheel of our inner life in his hands.

We are not concerned here with categorizing sin but with acknowledging the fact that the artifices

of the devil – the sovereignties of darkness the
New Testament writers speak of – are indeed real
forces. When we recognize this we can turn to
Christ's wonderful words about his promised victory: "When I drive out demons through the Holy
Spirit, the kingdom of God has already come to
you."

VIII Suppression

THOUGH some evil thoughts can be easily dismissed (or overcome by a short prayer), others are much harder to expel. In the case of such "besetting" evil thoughts, our natural reaction is often suppression: to push the offending idea back down, deep into our subconscious, in order to rid ourselves of it quickly. But that never works. As Freud and countless others have shown, a suppressed thought will always resurface, just like a corked bottle that is pushed below the water but bobs up again as soon as it is released. The only alternative — to continue with the picture of the bottle — is to grasp it and throw it out of the water altogether. In other words, the most effective way to truly rid our mind of a suppressed thought is to face it squarely and reject it. (Obviously I cannot agree with Freud's

conclusion to the problem: that one should release
the tension by acting on the repressed thought.)

Baudouin illustrates the effects of suppression
with another metaphor:

> A leaf that falls into a stream (or a leaf we intention-
> ally drop into a stream) just where the water disap-
> pears into the ground…will come out again at the
> next opening, because the underground stream has
> faithfully carried it there, though during this journey
> it has been beyond the reach of any outside interfer-
> ence. In the same way, an idea that has been intro-
> duced into our minds (or that we ourselves have
> intentionally introduced) will produce its effects
> after longer or shorter subconscious development.

The water and the leaf symbolize our inner life.
When we place a positive image or idea into our
heart, it will remain in us and work in us until it
appears again in the flow of conscious thought.
The same is true if we give room to an evil

thought or image. It may be concealed for a long time by the subconscious, but then suddenly it is there, and its previously unnoticed effect on our inner life will also make itself felt.

In my counseling work I have met people who lived in such fear of evil thoughts or feelings that they constantly suppressed everything that arose in their minds. Some of these poor souls lived in such a state of inner tension that they panicked at the very thought of a tempting thought: they lived in constant fear of their own psyche.

No one can remain sane in such a charged situation for long. In fact, he will soon be no different from the neurotic, whose attempts to free himself only entangle him deeper, or the schizophrenic, whose attempts to resist (or escape) voices or hallucination often fortify these delusions. To use another illustration from the natural world: the inner life of such a person is like an over-inflated balloon which will eventually burst, releasing a whole wave of suppressed thoughts and feelings at once.

Again, we can find inner help out of this only by recognizing that we cannot overcome *any* inner struggle by means of our own will power. Therefore we must first relax and become inwardly quiet. Each of us knows, deep down, what we really want, and even if we feel confused and unhappy, we must try to re-focus on that longing. God loves us and wants to help us, even if this belief is repeatedly attacked by doubt. He can help us overcome our fears. We must also remember that it is futile to try to fight unwanted feelings with other feelings. None of us can straighten out our emotions, but we can trust in God. He knows our deepest heart, and he can set our hearts at rest:

> The Spirit helps us in our weakness...and intercedes for us with groans that words cannot express. And he

40   who searches our hearts knows the mind of the
          Spirit, because the Spirit intercedes for us in accor-
          dance with God's will (Rom. 8:26–27).

IX   Faith

THE ONLY answer to inner torment is faith in
God. It might sound simplistic, but faith *is* the
only point where light can break into our lives and
bring us redemption from evil. Like grace, faith is
a mystery and does not lend itself to explanation.
For someone who has not experienced its power,
it may seem distant or even unattainable.

Faith cannot be acquired by a decision of the
will: it is a gift from God. Yet it can be given to
everyone who seeks it. As Jesus says, "Seek, and ye
shall find." What counts here is trust. Faith is not
dependent on reason — on theories, theological
systems, or other intellectual explanations. It is
belief, precisely *in the absence* of these things. Mary
had reason enough to doubt the angel who came
to her from God, but instead she believed — "Here

am I, a handmaiden of the Lord" – and received the Word in her heart. It can be that simple!

Many people do believe at least on some level; they know of Christ, and their hearts tell them: here is someone I can trust. Yet each of us also knows feelings of fear and anxiety, and these often lead to a suspicion and reserve. Something in us seeks Christ, and at the same time, something in us holds us back and makes us unwilling to open ourselves to him fully. But that is just what we must do. Openness is the first step to faith.

God's love is always around us, whether we accept it or not. As Pascal writes in his *Pensées,* "You would not have sought me had you not already found me." These words ought to help us recognize, in all humility, that Jesus loves us before we love him. Even if we are unaware of it, he may already be at work in our hearts.

Of course, faith does not magically transform us: the Enemy is always there, and he will always try to seek out a person's vulnerable spots so as to bring about his or her fall. It is not enough to give Christ just what is good in us, nor is it enough to give him our sins and burdens only. He wants our entire selves. If we do not entrust ourselves to him completely, we will never find the full inner freedom and peace he promises us.

The blessing that comes with faith in Christ requires even more, however. It demands obedience: "He who believes in the Son has eternal life; but he who does not obey the Son shall not see life, for the wrath of God rests upon him" (Jn. 3:36).

Often, through fear, we bring on the subconscious suggestion of our own inability to find help. When Jesus said, "Unless you eat my flesh and drink my blood, you can have no life," even his close followers found these words too hard to accept, and many left him. But when Jesus asked the Twelve, "Will you also leave me?" Peter responded, "Lord, to whom shall we go? You have the words of eternal life. We have faith, and we know that you are the holy One of God." As long as we have this faith, we will find that Jesus can and will do everything for us, too.

In this regard I have always felt that the symbol of Christ's blood is all-important. The purification he offers is not a new teaching or dogma, but the possibility of a personal relationship with him. It is *life:* "I am the bread of life. Anyone who comes to me shall never be hungry, and anyone who believes in me shall never be thirsty" (Jn. 6:35). And: "Truly, truly, I tell you; whoever believes in me has everlasting life" (Jn. 6:47).

Most moving of all is John's description of the promise Jesus holds out to each of us through all time, no matter how bleak the outlook or difficult the road:

> On the last and greatest day of the festival Jesus stood and cried in a loud voice, "If anyone is thirsty let him come to me and drink. If anyone believes in

me, as Scripture says, streams of living water shall
flow from out his body"(Jn. 7:37–38).

Apart from Jesus we will find no peace. He remains there even for those who leave him, as did
many people in his time who found his words too
difficult to accept, and he remains there for us,
too, even in the dark hours when our faith wavers.
He frees us, not only for this life, but for eternal
life. Therefore we pray for ourselves and for every
man and woman, including those who do not believe: "Lord, help us. We need you, your flesh, your
spirit, your death and life – your message for the
whole creation."

X   Self-Surrender

IF WE BELIEVE that faith is a gift from God, it follows that for this gift to become ours, we must willingly receive it. And we must receive it *as it is given* — we cannot dictate the path it takes us or the way it might change our lives. In short, to receive faith in God, we must surrender all faith in our own power to bring about change: "His power is made perfect in our weakness" (2 Cor. 12:9).

In an ancient text known as *The Shepherd*, the early Christian Hermas uses a vivid parable to show us the necessity of dismantling our human power. He describes the Kingdom as a great marble temple in the process of being built, and each man or woman in the world as a potential building block. Those blocks that appear useful are chiseled by the master stonemason, and if they fit, they are used.

Those that do not must be discarded. To me, the picture has a simple but profound meaning: God is able to use us only insofar as we are willing to be chiseled for his purposes – that is, only insofar as we surrender ourselves in order to serve his needs.

What is true surrender? A person may yield to a stronger person, or an army to a stronger army. We may yield to God because he is almighty, or because we fear his judgment. None of this is full surrender. Only if we experience that God is good – and that he alone is good – is it possible to yield our whole heart, soul, and being to him willingly and unconditionally, and *out of love*.

My father once said about this:

It is hard to describe how power is stripped of us, how it must be dropped, dismantled, torn down, and put away…It is not easily attained and will not happen by means of a single heroic decision. It must be done in us by God. Yet this is the root of grace: the dismantling of our power. And only to the degree that it is dismantled can God work in us, through his Holy Spirit, and construct his holy cause in us...

Naturally, the first step we must take is to ask God to enter our hearts. It is not that he cannot or does not want to act without our asking, but that he waits for us to open our lives to him of our own accord. "Behold! I stand at the door and knock. If anyone hears my voice and opens the door, I will go in and eat with him, and he with me" (Rev. 3:20).

Many people wonder why God does not force his will on them, if he is so powerful. Yet that is simply how God is. He waits for our readiness. It is true that he punishes those he loves and calls them to repentance; but he never forces his goodness on them.

If a father were to take his child by the throat and force his good intentions on him, the child would instinctively feel that this was not love. For the same reason, God does not force his will on anyone. So we are confronted by a momentous question: are we willing to surrender ourselves to God voluntarily – to open the windows of our hearts so that his goodness can enter and fill our lives?

To be sure, the struggles we have concerned ourselves with in this book make it clear that such surrender is never easy, but takes place against a backdrop of powerful forces. Jesus himself had to fight so hard to surrender his will to the Father's that he sweated drops of blood. Evil surrounded him on all sides, yet he remained faithful: his attitude was "Not my will, but your will." This should be our attitude too.

Often the most difficult situations – unexpected tragedy or death, suffering or sudden loss – will arise in life without our understanding why. It is the same in the struggle against sinful thoughts. Just when we are sure the battle over this or that obstacle has been won, we may be newly attacked. Even then, the answer lies in full surrender to Jesus.

Everyone is bound to go through hard times, and for some, the struggle to accept hardship will seem insurmountable. Yet we should never forget that the final victory belongs to God: "Heaven and earth shall pass away, but a new heaven and a new earth are coming."

XI   Confession

JESUS SAYS in Matthew 6:22–24 that as long as we try to serve two masters, we live in darkness. How, then, can we find the singleness of heart that brings us into his light? First, we must see that our inner eye is pure, and not lowered by the shame of unconfessed sin. As long as we remain burdened by hidden guilt, we will never find full freedom or joy: the eye will stay sick, and so the whole body will remain in darkness.

Confession – the act of unburdening our sins to someone else in order to be freed of their weight – is simple enough to define, but never easy to practice. As Baudouin writes, "When we discover that we have created our own misery, this recognition contains something so humbling for us that we are reluctant to acknowledge it." He goes on, "Yet precisely because we have created our misery, it is essential for us to be absolutely truthful about our failings in order to find healing."

Despite the unmistakable advice we find in the Letter of James — "Confess your sins to one another" — many Christians today question the need for confession. Some dismiss it as too "Catholic" an idea; others emphasize the importance of a private personal relationship with God and argue that it is sufficient to bring our sins to him. But that is a poor argument: God already knows our sins (Heb. 4:13). Unless we move beyond merely recognizing our sins and acknowledge them *to another person*, we will not be relieved of their weight.

When our burdens are comprised of specific conscious sins, as is usually the case, these must be confessed without fail. Here the "absolute truthfulness" Baudouin advises is vital, for without it a truly clean conscience remains an impossibility. Sometimes, however, we may feel attacked by evil in a more general way, and be fearful that we might have given in to it or responded inadequately. If such anxiety persists, that too should be confessed. This does not mean digging into the subconscious for every little thing. Where God tells us through our conscience that something is wrong, we should admit it so that it can be forgiven. But the goal of confession should always be liberation, not increased self-concern. We want to find Jesus, not ourselves.

Faith and a good conscience are completely interwoven. If we do not heed the voice of our conscience, our faith will suffer shipwreck. And without faith, we lose the possibility of finding a pure conscience in the first place. That is why the Apostle says that the consciences of those who do not believe are not clean. It is bound to be like this, because without faith the conscience has nothing to hold on to.

Beyond this, it is clear that when we confess a sin to someone we trust and love, a new bond is created through our admission of guilt. Jesus attaches great weight to this bond, as indicated by his emphasis on community throughout the gospels: in fact, he promises that where two or three are united in his name, there he will be in the midst of them. To me, this unity means community – whether in the form of shared work or food, common prayer, or reading and reflection with a friend or spouse. The important thing is the strength – and safeguard against sin – that comes from fellowship. A solitary heart is one in great danger.

In and of itself, confession is no help. People pay good money to tell psychiatrists their sufferings and sins, and these psychiatrists use all sorts of therapy to help them quiet their distraught consciences. In the end, without remorse for the sins we reveal, confession remains a mere "dumping" of sin from one person to another and can have no redeeming effect.

With remorse – with the desire to truly undo the wrongs we have committed by turning away from them for good – confession becomes a joy. In casting off the veil that has kept our sin hidden, it removes the spell of secrecy. I have seen people change in an instant; people who came to me in such distress that their sin seemed to burden them physically, but who almost skipped away once they had everything off their chests.

Bonhoeffer describes this transformation in a wonderful way and shows us that it is more than an emotional thing, but something with eternal meaning:

> In the confession of concrete sins the old man dies a painful, shameful death before the eyes of a brother. Because this humiliation is so hard, we continually scheme to avoid it. Yet in the deep mental and physical pain of humiliation before a brother we experience the Cross of Jesus as our rescue and salvation.

56   The old man dies, but it is God who has conquered him. Now we share in the resurrection of Christ and eternal life.

XII Prayer

FROM the Gospel of Matthew to the Book of Revelation, the New Testament is filled with references to prayer as the best weapon for the spiritual fight. One of the deepest of these is found in Ephesians 6:

> Find your strength in the Lord, in his mighty power. Put on all the armor which God provides, so that you may be able to stand firm against the devices of the devil. For our fight is not against human foes, but against cosmic powers, against the authorities and potentates of this dark world, against the superhuman forces of evil in the heavens. Therefore, take up God's armor; then you will be able to stand your ground when things are at their worst, to complete every task and still to stand. Stand firm, I say. Fasten on the belt of truth; for coat of mail put on integ-

rity; let the shoes on your feet be the gospel of peace, to give you firm footing; and, with all these, take up the great shield of faith, with which you will be able to quench all the flaming arrows of the evil one. Take salvation for helmet; for sword, take that which the Spirit gives you – the words that come from God. Give yourselves wholly to prayer and entreaty; pray on every occasion in the power of the Spirit (Eph. 6:10–18).

Another important passage is Matthew 6:16, where Jesus teaches us *how* to pray: he tells us to lock ourselves in our rooms and pray in secret so that God, who sees in secret, will reward us. I have always felt that Jesus' concern was not so much privacy as humility: he warns us against parading our piety before others "like the Pharisees," and against reciting long prayers.

Even with these reassuring words, a meaningful prayer life can still be elusive for a person engaged in an intense struggle against sin. A man I once counseled many years ago longed to find relief in his battle with a certain besetting sin, but simply could not find peace. This man prayed fervently for hours. When that didn't seem to help, he prayed for Jesus to free him from whatever subconscious resistance there might be within him. The more he prayed, the more confused and desperate he became, and his inner turmoil seemed to prove to him that his prayers were not pleasing to God.

How can such a person find help? Every case will be different, but in this instance a general truth seemed to hold: When we feel that our prayers are not answered, we should consider whether it isn't so much a matter of God not responding, as our own unbelief. Through autosuggestion, a feeling of doubt in God's power takes root in our mind, and the harder we thrash, the faster we sink in the paralyzing quicksand of helplessness. The answer is to stop thrashing and to listen for God's voice.

Too often we pray only for what *we* desire and forget to ask God what *he* wants of us at a particular moment. We forget the mystical wisdom expressed by Jesus in the words, "Blessed are the poor in spirit" (Mt. 5:3). Poverty of spirit means emptiness and silence, honesty and humility; it has nothing to do with the tenseness or turmoil of churned-up emotions. It means readying ourselves for God *as we truly are* — as poor, wretched sinners — rather than "fixing ourselves up" for him.

God knows our inner state, and there is little use in trying to improve its appearance. Clearly, fixing ourselves up is nothing but foolishness. So is trying to imagine how God wants us to be, and hoping that by entering a godly frame of mind he is more likely to hear and answer us.

Do not be anxious about anything, but in everything, by prayer and petition, and with thanksgiving, present your requests to God. And the peace of God, which passes all understanding, will guard your hearts and minds in Christ (Phil. 4:6–7).

God will always answer a genuine prayer, though he may not respond right away. Daniel prayed earnestly for the forgiveness of Israel's sins, yet received no answer for three weeks. Then an angel appeared to him in a vision and said:

> Do not be afraid, Daniel, for from the very first day that you applied your mind to understand and mortify yourself before your God, your prayers have been heard, and I have come in answer to them. But the evil angel prince of the kingdom of Persia resisted me for twenty-one days, until Michael, one of the chief princes of heaven, came to help me (Dan. 10:12–14).

So Daniel's prayers *were* heard from the beginning, though dark powers made it difficult for the angel who answered him to break through. Today, despite the victory of the cross, there are still dark powers at work. Our prayers, like Daniel's, may often not be answered straight away. Yet God hears them. Let us firmly believe this.

XIII   Detachment

WHEN, in the middle of a trying struggle, we feel a desire for God in the depth of our hearts, it is a sign that he *is* still there. (The fact that we are even struggling is a sign of this, too.) We may not have strength to follow him at that moment, but as long as we hear him through the voice of our conscience, we can hold on to that and know that he will lead us out of our struggle.

God is concealed deep within the heart of every human being, for each of us is made "in his image." If we have childlike faith in this, it should not be hard to believe that it is he whose voice directs us out of the darkness to freedom and light. Yet how, against the clamor of other voices that vie for our attention, can we find the inner quiet we need in order to hear him?

In one of his poems, my father touches on this question and speaks, in answer to it, of his longing to be "outpoured" for God so that he can await Him "in stillness." This stillness, which the 13th-century German mystic Eckhardt calls "detachment," is a daily necessity for every Christian. Detachment means separating ourselves from all the tensions of the day – from worries about work, leisure, and personal life; from the news, from sports, from headaches over practical problems, from the distractions of tomorrow's plans. It means standing before God in silence so that we can perceive his working in our hearts.

Even the "cramped will" I wrote of earlier must be yielded so that the deeper voice of the heart can speak without having to compete with anything else. This means detachment from mammon, impurity, and malice; from deceit, mistrust, and hatred; from all spirits foreign to God. Here I would like to emphasize once again the significance of the subconscious and remind the reader that the cause of an attack by an evil spirit is often found there. With this in mind, it should be obvious how important it is to find detachment every evening before falling asleep. Whatever we give room to in our heart may work on in us all night long.

We know we cannot achieve true detachment in our own strength, but that is no cause for self-doubt or worry. In fact, the best way to remain mired in struggle and to experience nothing good at all is to keep taking stock of our own weakness. I have counseled people who did this — they were so intent on watching themselves that they were always tense, and never able to listen to God.

If we really desire God's help, we should not look to ourselves, but to him. Eckhardt writes:

Nothing but the giving up of his will makes a true man. This alone is the perfect and true will, that one enters into God's will and is without self-will. For the whole perfection of man's will means being in harmony with the divine will, by willing what God wills.

At the time when the angel appeared to Mary, nothing she had ever done would have made her the mother of Jesus; but as soon as she gave up her will, at that same hour she truly became mother of the Eternal Word and conceived Jesus.

God has never given himself (nor will he ever give himself) to an alien will. Only where he finds his will does he impart and leave himself, with all that he is. This is true inner detachment. Then the Spirit stands immovable in the face of everything that befalls it, whether it is good or bad, honor or disgrace or calumny, just as a broad mountain stands immovable in the face of a little breeze.

The just man hungers and thirsts so very much for the will of God, and it pleases him so much, that he wishes for nothing else and desires nothing different from what God decrees for him. If God's will were to please you in this way, you would feel just as if you were in heaven, regardless of what happens or does not happen to you. But those who desire something different from God's will get what they deserve: they are always in misery and trouble; people do them a great deal of violence and injury, and they suffer in every way.

We deafen God day and night with our words, "Lord, thy will be done." But when God's will does happen, we are furious and do not like it a bit. When our will becomes God's will, that is certainly good; *but how much better it would be if God's will were to become our will!*

As it is now, if you are sick, of course you do not want to be well against God's will, but you wish that it were God's will for you to get well. And when things are going badly for you, you wish that it were God's will for you to get along better! But when God's will becomes your will, then if you are ill – it will be in God's name! If your friend dies – it will be in God's name!

Anyone who by God's grace unites his will purely and completely with God's will has no need other than to say in ardent longing: "Lord, show me what thy dearest will is, and give me strength to do it!" And God will do this, as truly as he lives, and to such a one he will give in great abundance and all perfection.

There is nothing a man is able to offer God that is more pleasing to Him than detachment. God cares less for our watching, fasting, or praying than for it. In short, God needs nothing more than this: *that we give him a quiet heart.*

For those whose severe temptations still confuse them and keep them from detachment, it may help to remember that the mind is never a blank void. Whatever we remove, we must replace. Therefore it is critical to not only drop everything that distracts us, but to focus our inward eye and ear on Jesus alone. The more we are able to look outward and forget ourselves, the more easily our mind can be

freed and healed by God. As the writer of Philip-
pians advises:

> Whatever is true, noble, right, or pure; whatever is
> lovely, admirable, excellent, or praiseworthy – think
> on such things...And the God of peace will be with
> you (Phil. 4:8–9)

When the soul finds this peace and is no longer
subject to the force of spirits warring within; when
it is no longer subjected to any force – not even
the pressure of its own tortured longing – then the
voice of God, which is the Spirit, can speak.

XIV   Repentance and Rebirth

WE HAVE discussed, in the previous chapters, the importance of self-surrender, confession, prayer, and detachment. These things aside, we are left with an all-important question: What must we do to make a complete break with the sin in our hearts, so that we can be "born again?"

According to the New Testament, we must repent. That is, we must not only acknowledge our sins, but show such deep and genuine remorse for them that we cut ourselves off from their power completely. Repentance is not a welcome idea among many believers today; as a whole, people squirm when confronted with it. No one likes to see himself as a sinner; it is nicer to be a good Christian. Yet don't all four gospels make it clear that Christ came for sinners — not for saints — and that the way to Christ is humility and poverty of spirit, not human goodness?

When the apostle Paul speaks of himself as "the greatest sinner," one feels these are not just pious words. He really meant them. Paul had persecuted the church and was responsible for the martyrdom of many believers; he knew he was an enemy of God. In the same way, at Pentecost, the people of Jerusalem saw themselves as sinners. They did not feel they were worthy of the Holy Spirit – far from it. They were "cut to the heart," and spoke of themselves as the murderers of Christ. But because of this recognition, God could use them.

If we want to be used by God, we must recognize that each one of us, too, is a sinner. Even Peter, one of the most trusted disciples, was humble enough to recognize his failings: after denying Jesus, we are told, he went away and "wept bitterly." There is no other way for us either, than to weep for our sins.

Repentance is not an easy thing: it demands hard struggle. Yet even in the darkest, most agonizing hours of soul-searching, we can take comfort in the fact that Jesus (though he was without sin) has been there before us. As we read in Hebrews:

> In the days of his earthly life he offered up prayers and petitions, with loud cries and tears, to God who was able to deliver him from the grave. Because of his humble submission his prayer was heard: son though he was, he learned obedience in the school of suffering, and, once perfected, became the source of eternal salvation for all who obey him… (Heb. 5:7–10).

Which of us takes our struggles with sin so seriously that we fight with loud cries and tears? Jesus did. No one has ever had to fight like him — no one. The devil wanted no heart more than his. And because he fought much harder than any of us will ever have to, he understands our struggles. We can be sure of that. Yet we will always have to fight, and that is why he says that those who want to follow him must take up their cross as he took up his.

Repentance does not mean self-torment. It may turn our lives upside down — in fact, it must — and at times we will feel as if the entire foundation has been swept away from under our lives. But even then we must not see everything as hopeless or black. God's judgment is God's goodness, and it cannot be separated from his mercy and compassion. Our goal must be to remove everything that is opposed to God from our hearts, so he can cleanse us and bring us new life — that is, so he can fill us with Christ.

It is a wonderful gift when a person truly repents. A heart of stone becomes a heart of flesh, and every emotion, thought, and feeling changes. One's entire outlook changes, because God comes so close to the soul. Sadly, many Christians resist repentance and rebirth. Others, even if they may not resist it, never experience its blessings because they do not seek it. They may be aware of sin in their lives, and at a certain level they may struggle in vain, year in and year out, to overcome it. Underneath, however, they feel trapped. They feel their sins are really just "natural," insurmountable human weaknesses, and so they resign themselves to this.

On the one hand, I have great compassion for such people; on the other, I feel their excuses are wholly indefensible. If I insist that I am too great a sinner – if I doubt that Christ can really help me – I hinder grace and prevent the Holy Spirit from entering my heart, because I am in actual fact doubting the victory of the resurrection. This doubt must be rejected. After all, Christ's power lies in this: that he carried the sin *of the whole world*, and yet overcame death (I Jn. 2:2).

Christ is always there, and so is the Holy Spirit, and if any soul cries out to God, it will be heard. It is not without reason that Christ calls himself our "Advocate:" there is no one who has as much compassion and love for sinners as he does, and he promises that "everyone who asks will receive... to him who knocks, the door will be opened." These promises are there for everyone. We cannot hide behind our sins and say, "I am too weak," or "I want to change, but I cannot." Ultimately, these excuses have no foundation.

Part of the secret of rebirth and new life is grace. Nicodemus' talk with Jesus shows that rebirth cannot be explained, but only experienced. Certainly we know it means the complete transformation of the old man into the new. But Jesus offers no rationale, no explanation. He simply says, "You must be reborn." For our part, then, we must simply believe that God wants to grant us new life.

Grace is the mysterious gift Christ gives each of us who turn to him. It is the key to rebirth and the possibility of a completely new life. It does not depend on merits or good deeds, but comes even to those who, humanly speaking, seem to deserve it least. As Paul says, it is "glorious and freely bestowed...Because we are one with Christ, we are released from bondage through his blood: our sins are forgiven. So rich is his grace!" (Eph. 1:6–7)

Through grace, Paul says further, "our sinful nature has no claim upon us" (Rom. 8:13). This is a very strong statement. Who can really say that the lower nature has no claim on him? Yet the answer to the riddle is clear, too: we must open ourselves to the power of the Spirit, repent, and dedicate our lives to Christ.

When we are ready, with every fiber of our being, to give him everything — to say, "Jesus, I am coming. I am coming, whatever the cost" — we will gain the assurance that sin can never be victorious in us, even though we may struggle with a particular weakness to our dying day. "There is no condemnation for those who are united with Jesus Christ, because in him the life-giving law of the Spirit sets us free from the law of sin and death" (Rom. 8:1–2).

xv   Healing

WE HAVE seen how, in our struggle against sin, we are often crippled by evil. Even when we have made what we thought was a firm decision to do what is right, the powers of suggestion and autosuggestion complicate the battle, confusing us, weakening our resolve, and sometimes overpowering us and leaving us with a feeling of complete helplessness. In German, the word *geisteskrank* — "sick in spirit" — is used to describe this state.

Like recovery from any illness, healing from such sickness of spirit takes time. Medicine is also needed — in this case, spiritual nourishment, inner nurturing, and the reassuring guidance of others. Ultimately, though, it is dependent on Jesus.

When I was thirteen years old, on a visit to the Wartburg Castle (about fifty miles from our home in central Germany), my parents showed me the study where Martin Luther translated the Bible into German. There was a large splotch of ink on the wall – Luther was tempted by Satan, they said, and hurled his inkwell at him to frighten him away. At the time I was very impressed, and left the room with the childlike notion that this is how a real man chases away the devil. Today I know that all the inkwells in the world can do nothing in the face of evil. If they could, the fight against sin in the human heart would be simply a matter of enlisting the will at the right time and place. We have seen that this never works.

Jesus alone can heal us and give us a new heart. He came to restore us through his blood, and every heart, however tormented, can find comfort and healing in him. In an essay entitled "The Conscience and its Restoration to Health," my father writes:

Jesus is the way to God. There is no other God than
the one who is the Father of Jesus. Wherever we may
seek him, we find Him in Jesus. Unless we are freed
in Jesus from all our burdens, we try in vain to draw
near to the Father of all, who is brought near to us as
our Father by Jesus. Without forgiveness of sin, we
have no access to God. Jesus gives it to us by sacrific-
ing his life – his body, his soul, and his blood.

The Accuser of our brothers is silenced; and the
conscience, too, is no longer allowed to accuse.
Even…the blood of the murdered brother, Abel, has
been erased. The better blood of the new Brother of
Man speaks louder than his. In him is found a new
representative and leader, who absolves and liberates.
Murdered like Abel, this Brother nevertheless speaks
for his murderers instead of against them because he,
though guiltless, has become one of them. He has
become the only one who is truly theirs. And if he,
the Son of Man, is for them, no one can condemn
them. From now on, no accusation has the power to
prevent them from approaching God.

This last sentence, about "approaching God," is very significant. It speaks of the action we must take if we want to find healing. For one person it might mean searching in silent prayer with outstretched hands; for another, running toward him in the sense of actively seeking him. But surely it cannot merely mean sitting there, waiting for Jesus to come and cure us with a magical touch! We must have expectant hearts.

The living spirit that God breathed into man at the dawn of creation remains in each of us only so long as we seek nearness to him and to our fellow human beings, and only if we fulfill the commandments that give meaning to these relationships: first, "Love the Lord your God with all your heart, with all your soul, and with all your mind;" and second, "Love your neighbor as yourself" (Mt. 22:37, 39).

Another vital part of healing after a struggle with darkness is the stand we take toward ourselves. The attitude we take to fluctuations of our imagination, for instance, can influence our entire emotional outlook. Obviously, the person who is aggressive — who is decisive and vigorous in fighting whatever must be fought — will be surer of victory than one who cowers in fear or self-protection.

As my father indicates in the passage above, the conscience is often our "accuser," and rightly so. Yet once we have unburdened ourselves and turned away from sin, its voice must give way to the voice of love — to the voice of Jesus. Thus Tolstoy warns, "If we reason about love, we destroy love." In other words, if we desire the healing of the will, we must be careful not to analyze every feeling that goes through our mind and destroy the new freedom wakening there.

It is fruitless to worry endlessly about our small hearts or our weak characters. No one is pure and good except Jesus; his is the only really healthy character. Let us turn our back on the temptation of Cain, who envied his brother's closeness to God. Let us become like little children, and find joy in simply belonging to Jesus.

When, after the initial victory over sin in our hearts, we still feel unsure of ourselves, it may be a sign that we do not yet believe deeply enough. Paul writes that if we love fully, we will understand as we are fully understood (I Cor 13:8–13). John's words are important, too: God loved us before we were ever able to love him (I Jn. 4:19). This is what must enter our small hearts, and what we must hold on to: the love of the great Heart which understands us fully.

In my experience, the road to healing is long,

and at one time or another every one of us will
have to endure disappointment and failure. Sometimes it will happen that we fall back into the sin
we dreaded most or were most certain of having
conquered. Yet in spite of the despair that follows,
we should not lose confidence, for "he who began
a good work in you will carry it on to completion
until the day of Christ Jesus" (Phil. 1:6).

The agonizing pain and loneliness Christ must
have felt as he hung on the cross is too fearful to
imagine; yet even then he cried out, "Father, into
thy hands I give my spirit." Here we find the crown-
ing of faith. Even the most intense suffering and
feelings of godforsakenness could not sway his faith
in his and our Father: he gave his spirit into God's
hands.

If we want to be healed of the wounds made by
Satan's tricks and arrows, we must find this same
unyielding trust in God, so that even if we feel

nothing yet, we are able to give ourselves absolutely and without reserve to him with all we are and have. Ultimately, all we have is our sin. But if we lay it before him like children, he will give us forgiveness, cleansing, and peace of heart; and these lead to a love that cannot be described.

XVI Purification

WHEN WE have just experienced true repentance and rebirth, a clean conscience and a pure heart are living realities, and the joy and conviction they bring may carry us for many days. For most people, though, struggles soon resume, and even if they are new, or less intense – even if we do not return to old sinful habits – we feel less and less able to speak of our purity with confidence. Faced with this knowledge, it is no wonder that many Christians simply give up believing in the possibility of true healing and a pure heart.

Is purity a practical goal, or just a wonderful ideal? In struggling to answer this vital question over many years, I always find myself returning to the one who calls us to a pure heart in the first place. If Jesus – the only sinless man to have ever walked the earth – struggled with temptation, how much understanding he must have for our lapses and failings! Yet he still demands of us, "Be ye perfect" and tells us that only the pure in heart will "see God."

The Swedish writer Selma Lagerlöf tells the story of a knight who, having lit a candle at the tomb of Jesus on one of the Crusades, vows to bring back this flame, unextinguished, to his home town in Italy. Though robbed by highwaymen and met by every possible calamity and danger on his journey, the knight is set on one thing only: to guard and protect his small flame. At the end of the story, we see how single-minded devotion transfigures this knight completely: having left home a ruthless warrior, capable of the worst deeds, he has returned a new man.

If, like this knight, we set our heart on one thing alone, we too can be wholly transfigured: "When he appears we will be like him, and we shall see him as he is. Everyone who has this hope in him purifies himself, just as he is pure" (1 Jn. 3:2–3). But as long as we remain divided, we will (to quote my father's book *Inner Land*) also remain "weak, flabby, and indolent; incapable of accepting God's will, making important decisions, and taking strong action... Purity of heart is nothing else than the absolute integrity needed to overcome enervating desires."

Before we dismiss this "absolute integrity" as another impossible ideal, let us look at what the apostle Paul says about purification. He takes it for granted that we will always have arguments and obstacles in our minds, and that we will always be subject to temptation. Yet he goes on to describe our fight against evil as a victorious one in which every thought is "taken captive to obey Christ" (2 Cor. 10:5). Again, the victory may not be easily gained. We must face the fact that the struggle is a full fledged war that has been waged continually since the fall of man, and that since the Resurrection and the coming down of the Holy Spirit at Pentecost, it has only intensified. The wonderful thing about Paul's words is his certainty that our thoughts *can* be taken captive to obey Christ.

In his writing "On Inner Detachment," Eckhardt tells us how a pure heart can become a reality for each of us:

If God is to enter into you, your creaturely, human nature must go out of you. For only where this nature ends does God begin.

God does not desire more of you than that you should go out from yourself, insofar as you are burdened with your human nature, and let God be *God* in you. The slightest image you have of the creature that you are, is as big as God: it keeps you away from your whole God. To the extent that such an image enters you, God must yield, and to the extent that this image goes out, God enters in.

Self-love is the root and cause of all evil; it snatches away all that is good and all that is perfect. Therefore if the soul is to know God, it must also forget itself and lose itself. For as long as it sees itself, it will not see and know God. But when it loses itself for God's sake and leaves all things, then it finds itself again in God because God dawns upon it — and only then does the soul know itself and all things in God...

Anyone who lets go of things in their trivial and incidental nature will possess them in their pure, eternal nature. Whoever has let go of them in their lower nature, in which they are perishable, will receive them again in God, in whom they have their true being...

It is an unmistakable sign of the light of grace when someone turns of his free will away from the transitory toward the highest good — God. Such a soul does not seek outside itself, but in the school of the heart, for it knows that there the Holy Spirit teaches it the things that lead to its blessedness…

It tries to do all its works as perfectly as possible in accordance with God's will…and strives always to have a clear conscience by disdaining worldly doings and loving suffering, so that grace may increase in it and the evil desire of the flesh may decrease.

When people hear the word "flesh," they tend to think right away of their sexuality, or perhaps excessive food and drink. But that is not the only meaning of the word. Certainly, sexual immorality and gluttony are "of the flesh," but so is self-righteousness, hypocrisy, and everything else in us that is of the ego — everything that is not of Christ. Purification means asking God again and again for help in overcoming the flesh — in particular, our spiritual pride. Pride is the worst form of the flesh, because it leaves no room in the heart for God.

If we look at ourselves honestly, we must humbly admit that each of us is in daily need of God's forgiveness. Our human weakness is no hindrance to the kingdom of God, however, as long as we do not use it as an excuse for our sins. Paul even writes that "the Lord will show himself in the most glorious way through our weakness" (2 Cor. 12:7–9).

In the end, then, purification depends on our readiness to dedicate our lives to God; and when we stumble or fall, to get up and dedicate ourselves anew. We will never be perfect, but we will always remain focused on our goal, and give everything we have to reach it:

> Not that I have already obtained all this, or been made perfect; but I press on to take hold of that for which Christ took hold of me...Forgetting what is behind and straining toward what is ahead, I press on toward the goal to win the prize for which God has called me heavenward...(Phil. 3:12–14)

XVII The Cross

IN EVERYTHING I have said so far about the struggle to overcome evil thoughts and feelings, my main concern has been to lead the reader to Christ and the cross. Each of us must find the cross. We can search the whole world, but we will find forgiveness of sins and freedom from torment nowhere except there.

Every believer knows that Christ went the way of the cross for our sakes. But it is not enough just to *know* this. He suffered in vain unless we are willing to die for him as he died for us. Christ's way was a bitter way. It ended in a victory of light and life, but it began in the feeding trough of an animal in a cold stable, and passed through tremendous need: through suffering, denial, betrayal, and finally, complete devastation and death on a cross.

If we call ourselves his followers, we must be willing to take the same path.

Christ died on the cross to break the curse of evil and vanquish it for once and for all. If we do not believe in the power of evil, we cannot comprehend this. Until we realize that the main reason for his coming to earth was to do this *on our behalf* — to free us from the powers of darkness — we will never fully understand *our* need for the cross.

The image of a sweet, gentle Savior, like the thought of an all-loving God, is surely wonderful, but it is only a small part of the picture. It insulates us from the real power of his touch. Christ comforts and heals, saves and forgives — we know that; but we must not forget that he judges too. If we truly love him, we will love *everything* in him; not only his compassion and mercy, but his sharpness too. It is his sharpness that prunes and purifies.

Christ's love is not the soft love of human emotion, but a burning fire that cleanses and sears. It is a love that demands self-sacrifice. My father writes:

> The Earth can be conquered in no other way than through sacrifice. Satan can be vanquished in no other way than through the Lamb. Jesus is the sacrifice who, being perfect, has been victorious over evil. In the sacrificial love of a lamb, Jesus has overcome the dragon, disarmed Satan and smashed his weapons on the cross. Thus it is impossible for Satan to prevail, with his instruments of darkness and death, against anyone who is one in faith with the crucified Christ.

Here we see that if Christ's freedom is to become ours, we must be one with the *crucified* Christ. His cross is the center, the linchpin, of the struggle between God and Satan, and as such it must become the center of our hearts too. In the cross alone is victory! In the cross alone is purity! It is there that the hosts of evil are overcome; that Christ's love to each human being springs eternal and gives us peace.

Unless these truths live in our hearts — unless they grip us in a deeply personal way and infuse our very being — they remain nothing but meaningless words. Jesus offers to give himself to each one of us to the extent that we become one flesh and blood with him. This is not a philosophy, but real food; it is life. It will change *everything* for someone who experiences it, and not only for that moment but for all eternity.

When we know Jesus in the depth of our hearts, we will begin to realize (even if only to a tiny degree) what he went through for our sake. As we have seen, this means surrendering ourselves to him in prayer and quiet, confessing our sins to one another, and laying them before the cross in a spirit of repentance. Then he will accept us and

give us reconciliation with God, a clean conscience,
and a pure heart. In rescuing us from inner death
and granting us new life, his love for us will spill
over into our own hearts and give us a great love
for him.

Naturally it cannot end here, however. The experience of personal purification at the cross is vital,
yet to remain focused on that alone would be use-
less. Christ's love is so great, it must lift our minds
above our little struggles — and any preoccupation
with our own salvation — so that we can see the
needs of others, and beyond that the greatness of
God and his Creation. The cross is so much greater than the personal; it has cosmic significance, for
its power embraces the whole earth and more than
this earth!

There are secrets that only God knows, and the
crucifixion at Golgotha is perhaps the greatest of
them all. In his Letter to the Colossians (1:19–20)

Paul speaks of its mystery and says only that it pleased God to let his full nature dwell in Jesus and to reconcile to himself everything on earth and in heaven "through the shedding of his blood on the cross." At the cross, then, not only earth but also heaven and all the powers and principalities of the angel world will be reconciled to God. Certainly not we, and maybe not even the angels, will ever fully understand this. But one thing we know: Christ overcame death, the last enemy, and through this, something took place that continues to have power far beyond the limits of our planet.

XVIII Living for the Kingdom

ULTIMATELY, despite the strongest will, the best intentions, and the most intense striving and struggling, we can do nothing good without Jesus. Just as a branch can bear fruit only when it is connected to a living trunk or stalk, we can lead fruitful lives only insofar as we are connected to the Vine, which is Jesus. Yet Jesus is not content with our merely being attached to him.

True, we have seen that it is not possible to recognize the universal significance of redemption — the significance of the cross — without having experienced Jesus himself in our hearts. But if we content ourselves with this personal fellowship with Jesus, and do not sense the greater picture of his plan for us as minuscule parts of an endless universe, we have made our Christ a very small Christ.

It is not sufficient, I believe, to merely acknowledge and love Jesus as the friend of our hearts, as a Savior who brings us eternal fellowship with God. Surely he wants us to be filled with far more: the vision of his Father's great kingdom. It cannot be enough to overcome a besetting sin and then settle back complacently, feeling, I have won my little fight. I can be the most righteous person in the world, morally speaking, but if I lack love and concern for others, my heart is not yet pure. If I let my neighbor go hungry when I am well fed, I have not truly overcome sin in my life. Jesus wants us to suffer the injustice and need of the world together with him; to hunger and thirst for righteousness for all people; to witness to his way of love and justice and peace – to fight with him for the building up of a city on the hill.

Again, none of this is possible for us without the experience of personal rebirth. There is no question that every time a person is won for Christ,

the power of sin and darkness is broken in his or
her soul, and this is a victory for the kingdom of
God. But if we go no further than individually
edifying encounters with Jesus, we are missing the
greatness of his cause. My father writes in this
regard:

> For so many Christians, here is where their interest
> dies down. People seek constant confirmation of
> such grace as they have already received. Instead
> they should say, "This personal experience is given
> to me to help me find clarity about the complete
> Christ and about God's kingdom, a clarity that will
> make my life part of the life for his kingdom."

Perhaps that is why we are told to seek the kingdom of God and his righteousness *first:* so that
we might become worthy not only in the sense of
personal blessedness, but as fighters for his kingdom. Let us live more intensively in the expecta-

tion of the Lord! If we do not wait for him in every aspect of our life, we do not really wait at all. I ask myself every day: have I really hoped enough, fought enough, loved enough? Our expectation of the kingdom must lead to deeds.

At the end of the Sermon on the Mount, Jesus says, "Everyone who hears my words and does them will be like a wise man who builds his house upon a rock foundation." It is in *doing* God's will we prove our deepest will. No matter how confused or fickle our emotions, our heart's longing must remain sure: we will either hunger and thirst for Jesus, or we will avoid him. The difference is decisive for each of us for all eternity.

What a mighty thing it is to live for God's kingdom! Do not shrink back. Live for it; look for it, and you will find that it is so powerful it will completely overwhelm you — it will solve every problem in your life, and every problem on earth. Everything will become new, and each person will love the next in Christ. All separation and sin, all suffering and darkness and death will be overcome, and love alone will rule.

About the Author

WHEN Johann Heinrich Arnold (1913–1982) was six, his parents, Eberhard and Emmy, left their upper-class home in Berlin and moved to Sannerz, a village in central Germany. There, with a small circle of friends, they set out to live in full community of goods on the basis of Acts 2 and 4 and the Sermon on the Mount. It was a time of tremendous upheaval. The same post-war restlessness that drove his father, a well-known editor, theologian, and public speaker, to this leap of faith drove thousands of others to rise up against the rigid social and religious conventions of the period and seek new ways of life. These were Arnold's formative years, and the steady stream of young anarchists and tramps, teachers, artisans, and free-thinkers who came through the little community influenced him profoundly. All of them had abandoned the hypocrisy of a Christendom that had grown meaningless, and many felt drawn to the life of dedication and joy they found at Sannerz.

Arnold himself felt the call to follow Christ at the age of eleven. Later, as a young man, he committed himself to life-long membership in the church community, known by then as the Bruderhof, or "place of brothers." In 1938 he was chosen a "servant of the Word" (pastor), and from 1962 until his death he served as elder for the growing Bruderhof movement.

The flock in Arnold's care was not what one could call a typical church, and he was anything but a pastor in the conventional sense of the word. He did not have a charismatic personality, and he had no formal theological training. He was a true *Seelsorger,* or "spiritual guide" who cared deeply for the inner and outer well-being of the communities entrusted to him. And he served his brothers and sisters in the first place as an equal who shared their daily lives in work and leisure, at communal meals, business meetings, and worship services.

Arnold was called on to address every aspect of spiritual life, personal and communal. But there is a visible thread that runs through all he wrote: Christ and his cross as the center of the universe. Again and again, he insists that without meeting Christ personally — without being confronted by His message of repentance and love — there is no possibility of a living Christian faith.

Arnold's Christ-centeredness gave him an unusual courage to confront sin. He could not tolerate indifference to the demands of the Gospel. But just as he fought evil in others, he fought it in himself, and the fight was never against a person, but against sin. At times, this earned him the criticism of being too "emotional," but as he himself once asked, how can one who loves Christ be coolly detached when the honor of the church is at stake?

It was this, too, that enabled him to call for repentance so sharply at times: "Are we ready to let Christ's Word cut deeply into us, or will we repeatedly protect and harden ourselves against it? We do not realize how often we stand in God's way. But we can ask him to cut us with his Word, even if it hurts." With the same vigor and insistence that he called for repentance, however, he also strove for compassion and forgiveness. If anyone took seriously Jesus' injunction to forgive so that we may be forgiven, and to forgive seventy times seven, it was he.

As elder of the Bruderhof communities, Arnold spent many hours reading, re-reading, and prayerfully considering the contents of a daily flood of letters, and his answers illustrated the humility with which he responded. When he was asked a question, he counseled, comforted, admonished, and even sharply censured, but he never criticized or belittled anyone who turned to him. And though hundreds of people turned to him year after year, he always turned them onward – beyond their preoccupation with their sins or their personal holiness – to Christ.

Arnold knew well that he did not have all the answers. Often he said that he needed to think about a matter in question or wished to consider it in prayer, or simply felt he did not know what to do about it. Asked to explain a difficult verse, an apparent contradiction, or the meaning of a mysterious passage in the Bible, he might say, "I have thought about these words a great deal, but I do not fully understand them myself. Let us leave it to

God. Some day it will be revealed to us" – and he would not attempt an interpretation. Though widely read and entirely at home in the Old and New Testament, he was a man whose education was the education of the heart, whose knowledge was the knowledge of the human soul, and whose understanding of God's ways was born of his love for God, for Jesus, and for the church.

Most important, Arnold was able to listen: he listened to his brothers and sisters, he listened to friends, strangers, to critics, and most of all he listened to God: "I want to listen with my inner heart to the voice of God speaking through the brotherhood. I want to confess Jesus in our time. I want to be poor...spiritually poor. I want to be obedient and go where the church sends me, and to do God's will."

There are many aspects of Arnold's writings that one might consider at greater length – the overriding influence of his father, Eberhard Arnold; of the German pastors Johann Christoph and Christoph Friedrich Blumhardt and their vision of the kingdom as a present reality; or of Meister Eckhardt, whose mysticism is reflected in Arnold's own inclination toward the mystical. There are also Dietrich von Hildebrand, Friedrich von Gagern, and Charles Baudouin, whose books he read and referred to often. All of these writers give Arnold's message a breadth of vision that cannot be ignored — a vision that lifts our eyes from the pettiness of daily life to see greater realities we often ignore. To use his own words:

> What a great gift it would be if we could see a little of the great vision of Jesus — if we could see beyond our small lives! Certainly our view is very limited. But we can at least ask him to call us out of our small worlds and our self-centeredness, and we can at least

ask to feel the challenge of the great harvest that
must be gathered — the harvest of all nations and all
people, including the generations of the future.

Other Titles from Plough

A Plea for Purity
Sex, Marriage, and God
Johann Christoph Arnold
Thoughts on relationships, sex, marriage, divorce, abortion, homosexuality, and other related issues from a biblical perspective.

The Awakening
One Man's Battle Against Darkness
Friedrich Zuendel
At once a biography and a devotional, this gripping historical account opens a rare window on the reality of the age-old fight between good and evil, and the way this fight plays itself out in the lives of ordinary men and women.

Why Forgive?
Johann Christoph Arnold
Stories of real people scarred by crime, betrayal, abuse, bigotry, and war who have earned the right to tell you that forgiveness is the only way.

Be Not Afraid
Life, Death, and Eternity
Johann Christoph Arnold

Drawing on stories of real people, Arnold addresses the universal human fear of aging and purposelessness, and shows that even today, in our culture of isolation and death, there is such a thing as hope.

God's Revolution: Justice, Community & the Coming Kingdom
Eberhard Arnold

Topically arranged passages on the church, community, marriage and family issues, government, and world suffering.

Discipleship
Living for Christ in the Daily Grind
J. Heinrich Arnold

Thoughts on following Christ, topically arranged. Includes sections on love, humility, forgiveness, leadership, community, sexuality, parenting, suffering, salvation, and the kingdom of God.

Why We Live in Community
Eberhard Arnold
with two interpretive talks by Thomas
Merton. Inspirational thoughts on the basis,
meaning, and purpose of community.

The Gospel in Dostoyevsky
Edited by the Bruderhof
An introduction to the "great God-haunted
Russian" comprised of passages from *The
Brothers Karamazov*, *Crime and Punishment*, and *The
Idiot*.

To order, or to request a complete catalog, call
US: 1-800-521-8011 or 724-329-1100
UK: 0800 018 0799 or +44 (0)1580 88 33 44
or visit our website at www.plough.com